♡ TIKVAH LOVES GARY

Created by

Wozie

♡ TIKVAH LOVES GARY ♡

ISBN 978-0-9828013-1-4

Printed in U.S.A.

DARDA PUBLISHING
Cleves, Ohio
http://www.dardapublishing.com

♡ DEDICATION ♡

This book of cartoons is lovingly dedicated to my late father,

HARRY WOZNIAK

(SEPTEMBER 15, 1915–JUNE 7, 1983)

who always wanted to be a cartoonist and whose hope was to see me fulfill those dreams.

Without him, this book would never have been possible, for I was blessed to inherit his fabulous sense of humor and his cartooning DNA genes.

My greatest regret is that he never lived to see this work.

♡ ACKNOWLEDGMENTS ♡

How can this author even **begin** to thank all the people, who encouraged me to publish these cartoons which were originally done for psychiatric and therapeutic reasons? When the world gives you lemons, why not make lemonade ... right?

Usually, when someone laughs out loud at your endeavors, it causes you to want to give up and jump off a bridge ... except when it comes to cartooning. Laughing out loud at your work is the greatest compliment ever and so I want to thank all those souls who laughed out loud at my most serious endeavors while in progress.

There are also those individuals who told me that the theme of this work ... namely ... unrequited love, was a theme with which everyone could identify. Somehow, I must have touched a few broken strings of many tattered and torn hearts.

I want to thank my good friend (YES! I have a <u>few</u> friends!), Carolyn Donner, who also has supported my endeavors and also contributed some very funny ideas to this book. I want to thank her also for helping to format and proofread this book.

I want to thank Carla McKnight, a real sweet-heart, who consented to type the manuscript since me typing with my toes is sooooo much better than me typing with my fingers.

And, HOW could I ever forget to thank those great cartoonists whose work brought me great joy and tears of laughter. People like Charles Schulz, Kathy Guisewite, Johnny Hart, Morton Walker, Marge of Little LuLu, Dik Browne, Walt Kelly, Hal Foster, Walt Disney, Wally Wood, Will Elder, Jack Davis, and many others who had their work in comic books. To them I am very grateful as without them I probably would have never learned to read, much less draw cartoons.

And finally on a serious note, last but certainly **not** least, I want to thank the Creator of all things, who is a God of persistent and relentless love. He has taught me that love is eternal and stronger than death and that love **never** gives up even though loving also brings great pain and suffering as in the paraphrased words of C. S. Lewis, "love and suffering go together ... THAT'S THE DEAL!"

But in the end, it is worth it!

I thank each and every one of you, and may God bless you all.

Wozie

♡ PREFACE ♡

This is
Tikvah Ham.

THAT'S ME !!!

Her name implies
that she is always
hopeful that Gary will
love her. She wants a
long-term, loving
relationship with him.

She is emotional and expresses herself in no uncertain
terms. She is bold and brave and sometimes she stupidly gets
her foot into her mouth only to change it for the other foot.
Her love for Gary so overwhelms her that she can only keep
telling him over … and … over … and over like a broken record
or CD player.

This is Gary Tilden.

His name means "spear," a defensive weapon. He is always fighting Tikvah's advances and feels that he must defend himself. He has no clue how much Tikvah cares, yet he is very intelligent, logical and focused on his studies and his love for music. He is afraid of making any commitment as he does not want to be hurt.

Why he thinks Tikvah would ever hurt him is beyond anyone's logic or imagination.

And so we begin our saga of Tikvah ... and ... Gary ...

TIKVAH

TIKVAH

TIKVAH

TIKVAH

TIKVAH

TIKVAH

TIKVAH

DAVY CROQUET

1.

JAMES BEAN

2.

BRETT PITTS

(HE LOOKS LIKE JAMES BEAN)

3.

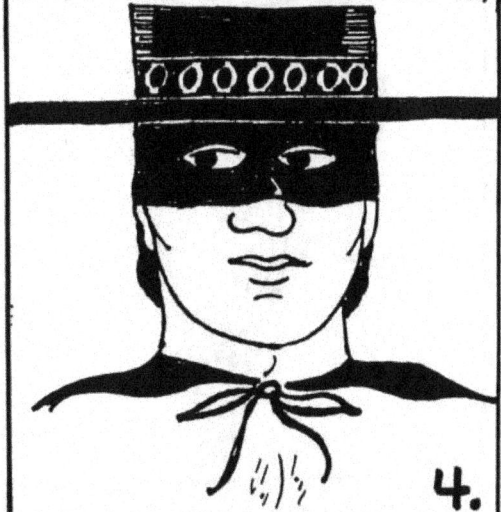

ZORRO
(ANTONIO BANDANAS)

4.

continued

JACK SWALLOW

5.

MICHAEL BUBBLY

6.

GARY TILDEN

7.

BOY.....IT'S HARD TO DECIDE......

8.

TIKVAH

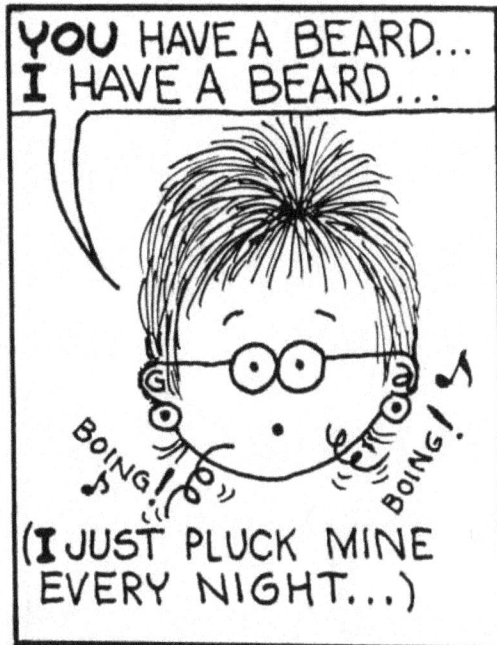

TIKVAH

Panel 1: THEY ARE TALKING AT THE SAME TIME, AND NEITHER ONE HAS HEARD WHAT THE OTHER HAS SAID.

Panel 2: WAIT...YOU GO FIRST. / NO, YOU GO FIRST. / NO...YOU GO AHEAD! / NO, YOU GO AHEAD.

Panel 3: NO...LADIES FIRST. / WELL, IF YOU INSIST... / ©Wozie

Panel 4: UH....GARY...I FORGOT WHAT I WAS SAYING! / I FORGOT WHAT I WAS SAYING, TOO...... / SOUL MATES......

YOU ARE MY SOUL-MATE, THE LOVE OF MY LIFE *

Verse 1:
There has never been a time - That I have ever felt like this.
Since that day you came and walked into my life -.
There has never been a time when I have felt such total bliss.
        You are my soul-mate - You are the love of my life.
        You are my soul-mate, You are the love of my life.

Verse 2:
As I sit here all alone - Remem'bring only your embrace,
I still hope that by my side you soon will be.
I close my eyes, I hear your voice, and then I see your loving face.
        Oh, dear love of my life, please come to me.
        You are my soul-mate, you are the love of my life.

BRIDGE:
You gently lead me through the lonely traces of your mind;
You take my hand so I would never linger far behind.
As we journey through the pathways, we often stop to eat and drink.
Then, I know that we are soul-mates, for as one, we always think.
You are my soul-mate - You are my soul-mate -
You are my soul-mate - You are the love of my life.

Verse 3:
Above all else, you are the only, only one I'm thinking of.
Oh, my only love, you'll always, ever be.
There is not another person I could really ever love,
For you are just every single thing to me!
You are my soul-mate, You are the love of my life!

YOU ARE MY SOUL-MATE, THE LOVE OF MY LIFE *
(continued)

BRIDGE:

You're the one I've always hoped for, No one else, I'd ever find!
There will never be another, There's only you, one of a kind.
I've seen the world and many places, and this I know is true:
In all the earth there is no other as so wonderful as you!
You are my soul-mate – you are my soul-mate!
You are my soul-mate - You are the love of my life!

Vs 4

I will always love you, darling, until the day I die.
To the love of my life I will be true –.
For you are my loving soul-mate – And to you I'd never lie.
I will always love and cherish only you!
You are my soul-mate, You are my soul-mate,
You are my soul-mate, You are the love of my life!

*Music available from Darda Publishing

TIKVAH

TIKVAH

TIKVAH

TIKVAH

TIKVAH

TIKVAH

TIKVAH

TIKVAH

TIKVAH

TIKVAH

IT WILL NEVER BE THE SAME *

Verse 1:
In the empty solitude was hopeless dreaming –
Of a love that never was, just fruitless scheming.
Then, in that cold and lonely night, 'Twas when you came into my sight;
And then, life finally had meaning. It will never be the same
Since that day when you came and brought me light.

Verse 2:
All the grief I had to bear brought floods of ceaseless rain.
But ever since that lovely day when, then you suddenly came,
All the torrents of my tears all dried up with all my fears,
And you were like the rainbow. My life has never been the same
Since that day when you came; This is very clear.

BRIDGE:
My heart aches so very much when I am apart from you.
I tremble at the very thought that you might love me, too.
Things have never been the same since the very day you came
Into my life. Oh, no! It will never be the same -
Never be the same again - This I surely know.

Verse 3:
As the lightning suddenly shatters the cold, dark, empty sky,
And the roaring sound of thunder slowly fades away to die –
Through the storms of the night it will never be right
Without you beside me. It will never be the same
Since the day that you came into my life.

IT WILL NEVER BE THE SAME * (continued)

Verse 4:

Please never, ever say to me that you will leave and have to go.

I could never exist because I love and need you so.

No, I will never be the same because into my life you came.

This is all I know – I will never be the same.

No – I'll never, ever be the same - Oh, no.

*Music available from Darda Publishing

TIKVAH

TIKVAH

TIKVAH

TIKVAH

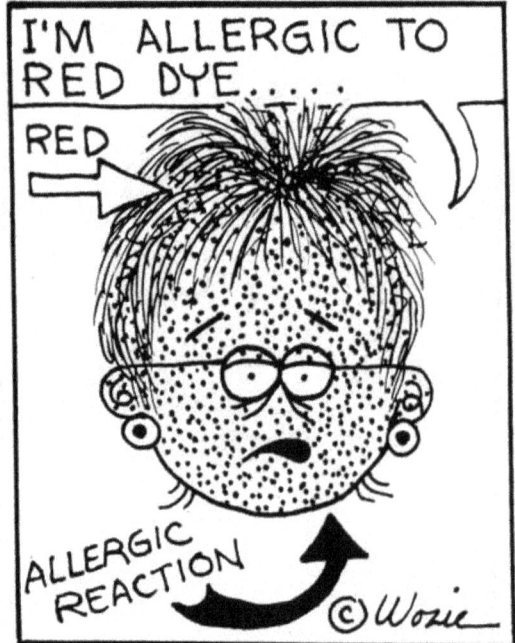

TIKVAH

TIKVAH

TIKVAH

TIKVAH

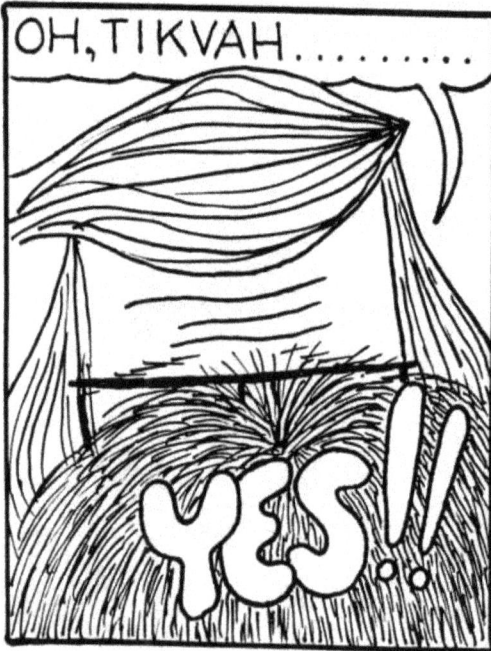

TIKVAH

TIKVAH

continued

46

TIKVAH

TIKVAH

TIKVAH

TIKVAH

TIKVAH

IN THE DISTANT TOMORROW *

Verse 1:
In the mist of the future I see you standing there, standing there;
I see the look on your sensitive face
    That shows me you care, you really care.
    Through all my tears and heartfelt cries,
    I see all the love in your tender eyes;
And I know that God has answered ev'ry prayer;
    For there I'll be – without sorrow.
    This I see – in the distant tomorrow.

Verse 2:
I see you standing alone in the distance
    Waiting for me – hoping for me.
I see your smile at the very instant
    When you see me, when you see me.
        I see your loving arms open wide
        As I run to be by your side;
And I feel your strong arms tightly wrap around me;
    For there I'll be – without sorrow;
        This I see – in the distant tomorrow.

BRIDGE:
In the distant future it appears so plainly in my mind,
As I wander through the vaporous mist, I know that you, I'll find
I hope and pray that some sweet day since your love I'm anticipating,
When I approach, I'll see you there as the clouds are all dissipating.

IN THE DISTANT TOMORROW *
(continued)

Verse 3:
Through the fog and the dew of the future
     I see you - shining through.
I see the joy written on your face
     When I say, "I still love you", yes, I do.
         Through all the sorrows of all the past,
         I know that you'll give love to last;
And I know that the love we'll share, will be true.
     And there I'll be - no fears to borrow.
     This, I see - in the distant tomorrow.

Verse 4:
Through the haze of the days to come,
     Your voice I hear, your voice I hear.
I hear your kind, tender words of love -
     It is so clear, so very clear.
         As I feel your warm embrace,
         And the touch of your hands on my face,
And you gently wipe away my ev'ry tear.
     Yes, then I'll be - without sorrow.
     This I see - in the distant tomorrow.

*Music available from Darda Publishing

TIKVAH

TIKVAH

TIKVAH

TIKVAH

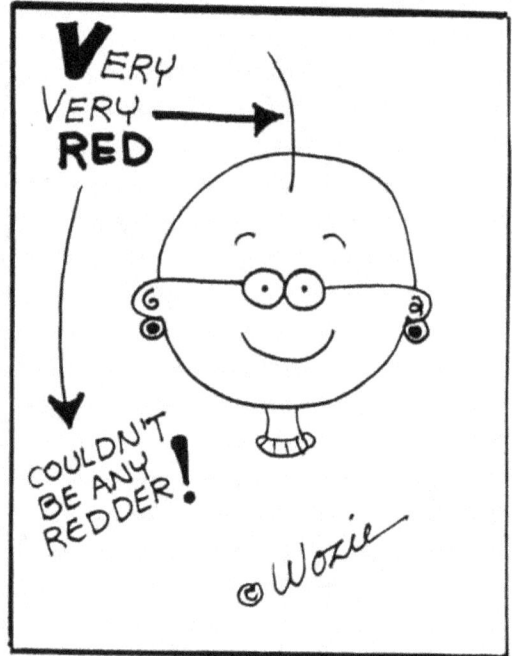

TIKVAH

59

TIKVAH

TIKVAH

TIKVAH

TIKVAH

TIKVAH

TIKVAH

I COULD NEVER SAY GOODBYE *

Verse 1:

I could never say-goodbye-to you.

I just can-not be-gin to try,- it's true.

> There is no reason that I should.

> There is no way I real-ly could -

> > Tell you - goodbye - I know that I'd die.

> I could never say goodbye.

Verse 2:

You came a-long that dark and lone-ly night.

I re-mem-ber how you - held me - so tight.

> I knew as we were standing there,

> You were the ans-wer to my ev-ery prayer.

> > I be-gan to love you so - How could I let you go?

> I could never say goodbye.

TROMBONE SOLO:
> BRAAH BRAAH BRAAH BRAAH
> > BRAAH BRAAH
> > BRAAAAAAAH
> > BRAA-BRAAAAAAAAAAAAAAH
> BRAAH BRAAH BRAAH BRAAH
> > BRAAH BRAAH
> > BRAAAAAAAH
> > BRAA-BRAAAAAAAAAAAAAAH
> BRAA BRAA BRAA BRAA BRAA
> > BRAH BRAH BRAAAAAH
> BRAA BRAA BRAA BRAAAAAAAAAAAAAAA
> > BRAH BRAH BRAH-BRAH
> BRAH BRAH BRAH BRAH BRAH BRAAAAAAAAAAAAA

I COULD NEVER SAY GOODBYE * *(continued)*

BRIDGE:
A sil-ly quar-rel almost tore – us apart.
We both knew that from the ver-y start
      We were only hurt-ing one-another.
      Should we say goodbye – to each other?
         Would I say goodbye to you?
         Would you say that we were thru?
Is that – what we – should – do –?
Oh – no! We should never say goodbye!

Verse 3:
You are the on-ly one who's meant – for me!
On-ly yours is who I want – to be!
      How could you ever real-ly know,
      That I could never let you go?
         It's you – I adore,
         For now – and ever-more.
I could never say goodbye.

TAG:
And I will never say goodbye!

*Music available from Darda Publishing

TIKVAH

TIKVAH

TIKVAH

TIKVAH

TIKVAH

TIKVAH

TIKVAH

TIKVAH

TIKVAH

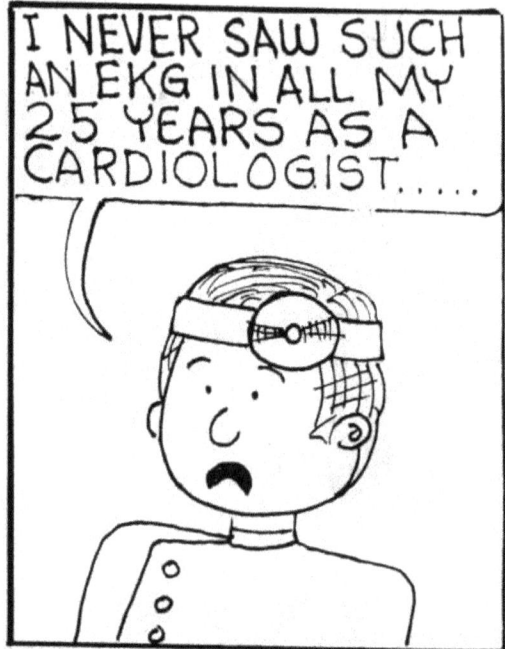

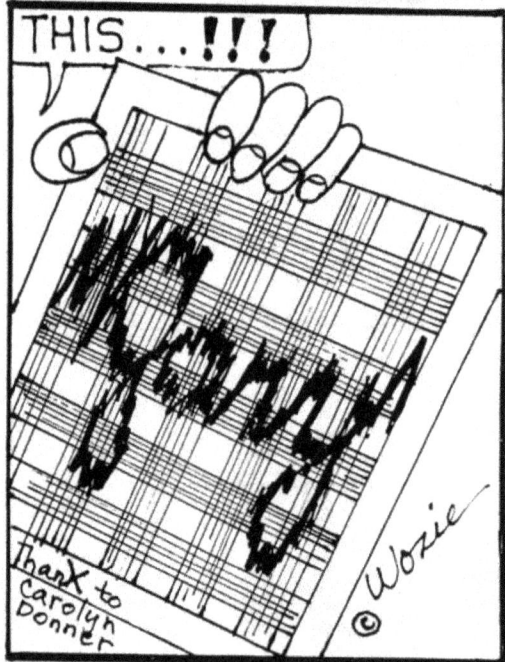

TIKVAH

Panel 1: PRESENTING THAT FAB DUO—TIKVAH HAM AND GARY TILDEN—DOING TIKVAH'S LATEST--- 1.

Panel 2: JAZZY COMPOSITION— "NOBODY BUT YOU"* WITH GARY ON HIS GOLDEN TROMBONE!! 2.

* AVAILABLE ON CD AT DARDA PUBLISHING CO

Panel 3: (INTRODUCTION--) BRAAH-BRAAH-BRAAH-**BRAAH**BRAAH-BRAAH BRAAH---BRAHBRAH BRAH**BRAH**BRAAAH--- 3.

Panel 4: BRAHBRAH BRAH— **BRAH** BRAH---BRAAAAH BRAH BRAH— BRAAAH-BRAAAA-BRAAAAAH—! 4.

77

NOBODY BUT YOU--
CAN TAKE AWAY
THIS PAIN---.
INSTRUCTIONS:
TAKE ONE
CAPSULE AT
BED-TIME.
21.
NOBODY BUT YOU--
WILL FILL MY LIFE
WITH RAIN--.
SAVE ME!
22.
NOBODY BUT YOU--
CAN GIVE ME
SUCH A HIGH--!
23.
I'M JUST AS
HAPPY AS CAN BE--
24.

84

TIKVAH

TIKVAH

TIKVAH

TIKVAH

TIKVAH

TIKVAH

TIKVAH

Panel 1: TIKVAH... YOU KEEP SAYING THAT YOU LOVE ME OVER AND OVER AND OVER...

Panel 2: HOW WOULD YOU LIKE IT IF SOMEONE WAS ALWAYS CHASING YOU AND TELLING YOU OVER AND OVER AND AGAIN AND AGAIN?? HOW WOULD **YOU** LIKE IT??!

Panel 3: ?
HUMMMMMM.....?

Panel 4: I WOULD JUST **LOVE** IT!

©Wozie

TIKVAH

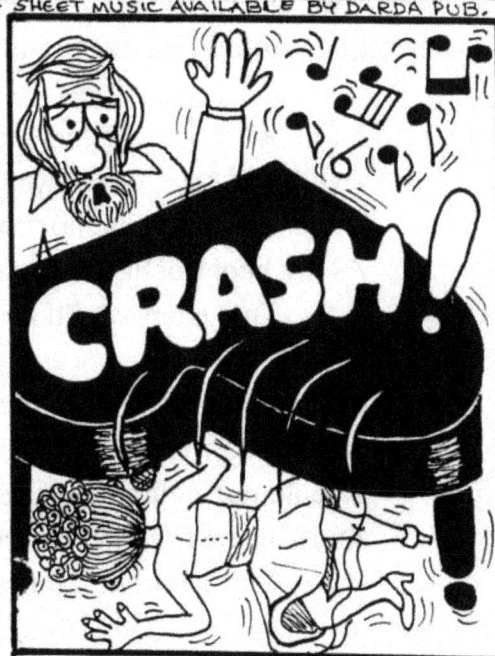

A MOMENT I'LL NEVER FORGET *

Verse 1:   There you stood all alone, - across the vast room,
And our eyes gently locked as they met.
I saw love in your face when you gave me that smile,
In a moment I'll never forget;
     Yes, a moment I'll never forget.

Verse 2:   As we walked out the door, then I felt your strong hand
On my waist in a sweet, gentle touch.
'Twas a moment in time, I shall never forget,
And that caused me to love you so much;
     In a moment I'll never forget.

Bridge: I will never forget how you looked at me
With eyes so tender and kind.
I will never forget that moment in time;
Each detail I've stored in my mind.

Verse 3:   I will never forget how your hand went in mine,
In a brief touch that was so sweet.
I shall always remember those chills down my spine,
As my heart ached, and then skipped a beat;
     In a moment I'll never forget.

Verse 4:   I found strength in your arms as they wrapped around me;
In that gentle embrace there was peace.
I could not help myself as I said, "I love you".
And I knew then my love would not cease;
     In a moment I'll never forget.

*Music available from Darda Publishing

TIKVAH

TIKVAH

TIKVAH

TIKVAH

* SHEET MUSIC AND CD AVAILABLE IN NEAR FUTURE BY DARDA PUBLISHING.

AND I WONDER IF YOU ARE DREAMING ABOUT ME--AS I DREAM OF YOU--
13.
DO YOU KNOW HOW MUCH I NEED YOU-- I REALLY DO---
14.
AS THE DAYS PASS BY-- AND WE ARE SO FAR APART;--I LONG FOR YOU--
25 26
27 28 29 30 31
15.
THEN THE TEARS ONCE AGAIN, LIKE RAIN-- BEGIN TO START-- YES, THEY DO---
CRACK!
HONK!
16.

TIKVAH

TIKVAH

TIKVAH

TIKVAH

TIKVAH

TIKVAH

TIKVAH

TIKVAH

TIKVAH

TIKVAH

TIKVAH

TIKVAH

TIKVAH

TIKVAH

TIKVAH

TIKVAH

TIKVAH

TIKVAH

Panel 1: TIKVAH, I HAVE TOLD YOU A 1000 TIMES... I DO NOT LOVE YOU, AND I NEVER EVER WILL. I DO NOT **LOVE** YOU NOW OR EVER. I DO **NOT** LOVE YOU. I DO NOT L-O-V-E Y-O-U. I NEVER EVER, EVER EVER WILL. NOT EVER!!?!!
BUT... EVER!

Panel 2: IT DOESN'T MATTER, GARY. I **STILL** LOVE YOU....AND I **ALWAYS** WILL... OH.... GARY!!

Panel 3: LATER: WELL, GARY, HAVE YOU ACTUALLY **TOLD** HER THAT YOU DON'T LOVE HER AND YOU NEVER WILL?

Panel 4: HUMMMM....YOU'RE RIGHT, JIM. MAYBE I JUST **HAVEN'T** BEEN DIRECT ENOUGH....
SIP!
© Woxie

TIKVAH

TIKVAH

MY LAST CHANCE FOR LOVE *

Verse 1:   I have never been – a gambling person;
            I always knew – the stakes were high.
            But when I fell – in love with you,
            My heart above – my head did fly.

            I gambled – only for your love,
            And from the start – I always knew –
            That I was taking – the biggest chance, Dear,
            When I wanted – only you!

BRIDGE 1:   How could – I know
            It was my last chance for love?
            For I need – you so,
            And my love for you could only grow and grow–!

            Please do – not leave;
            This is my last chance – for love.
            My heart – will grieve,
            For I will never love another, I believe!

Verse 2:   I had nothing – in the world to lose.
            Everything – is all I had to gain!
            I always thought – that I – would win
            And never have – to suffer any pain!

            Everything I had – I put into the till –
            My badly bruised – and battered heart.
            I never, ever – dreamed how slim
            My chances were–right–from–the very start.

MY LAST CHANCE FOR LOVE * *(continued)*

BRIDGE 2:   Please do not go! –
You are my last chance for love ! –
Why is this so?
For there will never be another love, I know.

What can I do? –
This is my last chance for love! –
Why is this true? –
'Cause I will never, ever find – another you! –

Verse 3:   You told me – that you would never love me
Tho' I gave – everything I had to you.
Long ago, – the deck was stacked against me. –
There was nothing – that I could ever do. –

Won't you please – give me a winning chance, Dear.
I can only offer you – my heart! –
Please tell me – that one day – you will love me,
And chances are – that we will never part!

BRIDGE 2: (REPEATS)

*Sheet music available from Darda Publishing

TIKVAH

TIKVAH

TIKVAH

TIKVAH

132

TIKVAH

TIKVAH

TIKVAH

AND I ALWAYS WILL *

Verse 1:   You said that my love – For you in time would die.
            How could you know, Love, – That every night I cry
            For you to see that – My heart is so sincere;
            And when I tell you that – My love is endless, Dear
            I love you still, – and I always will!

Verse 2:   You think that my love – Will surely slowly fade.
            You need to see that - My love is heaven-made;
            And what that means is – My love will never end.
            I'll love you forever, On that you can depend!
            I love you still, and I always will!

BRIDGE: I'll always love you – No matter what you say!
            I'll be thinking of you, No matter come what may.
            I'll always love you - Forever and a day!
            I love you still - and I always will!

Verse 3:   My love for you – Is the kind that only grows.
            It is a true love – That heaven only knows!
            My love for you – Is so beautiful and pure;
            It is the kind of love – That only will endure!
            I love you still! – And I always will!

BRIDGE : (REPEAT)

Verse 4:   You said that my love –   Would vanish in a year.
            Oh, my Darlin', Please don't ever fear!
            I'll always love you – 'Til poets run out of rhyme!
            I'll love you always – Until the end of time!
            I love you still! - And I always will!

*Music available from Darda Publishing

TIKVAH

TIKVAH

TIKVAH

TIKVAH

TIKVAH

TIKVAH

TIKVAH

143

TIKVAH

144

TIKVAH

145

TIKVAH

TIKVAH

TIKVAH

TIKVAH

WHY DID YOU SAY GOODBYE? *

Verse 1:   Sitting all alone in my chair,
          I keep wond'ring why you're not there.
    You left me, and now – you're gone. How can I ever go on?
    All I have – is – a memory – Of the way – it used to be!
    All my dreams have fled – and gone,
          Since you said goodbye to me.

Verse 2:   Ever since you said goodbye, All I ever do is cry.
    For there will never be – Anyone but you for me!
    No matter how hard I try, I can't find the reason why
    You said goodbye to me. - Why did you say goodbye?

BRIDGE: Why did you say – goodbye? – I still keep wondering why.
    What's so good about – goodbye – When I just want – to die? –
    This fact is very true: I'm alone and I still love you.
    Why did you ev-er say good-bye? Don't you know that I love you?

Verse 3:   I relive the moments we shared.
          Those were the times I thought you cared.
    How did things go – so wrong? Now, for – you I – do long.
    All I e-ver do is cry, And I always won-der why –
    Did you ev-er say good-bye? – How could you ever say goodbye?

Tag: All I ever do is cry - And I always wonder why -
    Did you ever say goodbye. How could you ever say goodbye?

Fadeout: All I ever do is cry! Why did you say goodbye?
    And I think I'm gonna die! Why did you say goodbye?
    All I ever do is cry, And I think I'm gonna die!

* Music available from Darda Publishing

TIKVAH

TIKVAH

TIKVAH

TIKVAH

TIKVAH

TIKVAH

TIKVAH

EVER SINCE GARY GOT SO MAD AT ME SEVERAL WEEKS AGO.....

I HAVEN'T HEARD FROM HIM AT ALL.

I DON'T KNOW, PAT.....

I GET THIS GNAWING FEELING THAT HE IS HIDING FROM ME...

TIKVAH

WHAT DID I MAKE YOU DO? *

Verse 1:   What did I make **you** do?
I just really don't have a clue.
If it's only just the same,
I just as soon make YOU the blame!

You kept tellin' me what I did wrong;
It's just the same ol' dance and song.
But this one thing is very clear;
I'm glad that you're no longer here.

Verse 2:   We were both two of a kind.
I know that you will really mind -
Me comparing me with you;
'Cause you just don't have a clue.

What in the world did I DO?
I don't even have a clue.
Yeh, it's so doggone true;
I love to keep on blamin' YOU!

BRIDGE: Our relationship was one for which to fight,
So we fought each other with all – our might!
'Twas a relationship for which one could die;
We almost killed each other, bye and bye … .

Verse 3:   What did I make you do?
I sure really wish I knew.
If it's all the same to you,
I wanna keep on blamin' YOU.

WHAT DID I MAKE YOU DO? *
(continued)

Verse 3 (continued):

       So instead of blamin' me,
       You really just need to see.
       It's not what I made YOU do;
       It's what YOU made ME do!

*Music available from Darda Publishing

ADVERTISING BLURBS:

"The BEST country song ever written!"

"Profound, yet VERY simple."

"Gets to the HEART of the matter."

"BEST RAP SONG ... WRAPS IT ALL UP ON WHO GETS THE RAP...!"

TIKVAH

TIKVAH

TIKVAH

TIKVAH

TIKVAH

FORGIVE ME *

Verse 1: Forgive me – for hurting you, my Love;
For-give me – it's you I'm thinking of.
For-give me, – please, – forgive me.

Verse 2: I'm sorry for saying what I said;
I real-ly – simply lost my head.
I'm sor-ry; please – for-give me.

BRIDGE:
I'm sor-ry that I hurt you by my foolish pride.
Please take me back; I need again to be – by your side.
My life is so empty; I am so alone and blue.
Please tell me that you'll take me back again to be with you.

Verse 3: For-give me – for what I did to you.
For-give me–you know my love is true.
Please tell me – that you'll for-give me.

*Music available frim Darda Publishing

TIKVAH

CONTINUED →

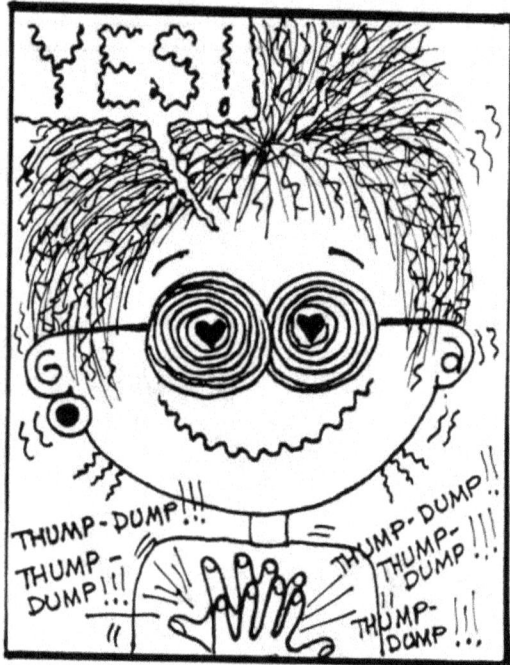

TIKVAH

Panel 1: INTRODUCING...TIKVAH SINGING HER VERY OWN COMPOSITION..."GARY", ARRANGED AND ACCOMPANIED BY GARY TILDEN.

Panel 2: (INTRODUCTION) PLINKITY--PLINK PLINKITY--PLINK PLINK PLINK

Panel 3: OH--GA-RY,--O DEAR GA-RY---

Panel 4: YOU'RE THE ONLY ONE I'M THINKING OF.---

176

The Dream Team...

www.ingramcontent.com/pod-product-compliance
Lightning Source LLC
Chambersburg PA
CBHW080555090426
42735CB00016B/3245